The Kid's Running Journal!

Getting Started on the Right Foot

SMARTER JOURNALS AND NOTEBOOKS

Smarter
Journals and Notebooks
JOURNALS AND NOTEBOOKS

Copyright 2016

Good Tips For Losing Weight
Health Infographics

Drink a lot of water

Don't Miss Breakfast

Have 5 Food Groups

Cardio every day

7-8 hours Asleep

Don't eat Junk Food

LESSONS

....
....
....
....
....
....
....

Date _____

Training distance _____

Time run _____

Location _____

Who you ran with _____

weather _____

How did you feel

Goal Complete?

Yes ○   No ○

Good ○
Tired ○
Sore ○
fatigued ○

Notes

....
....
....
....
....
....
....
....
....

....
....
....
....

Date _____

Training distance _____

Time run _____

Location _____

Who you ran with _____

weather _____

How did you feel

Goal CompleteD?

Yes ○   No ○

Good ○
Tired ○
Sore ○
fatigued ○

Notes

....
....
....
....
....
....
....
....
....

....
....
....
....

Date _____

Training distance _____

Time run _____

Location _____

Who you ran with _____

weather _____

How did you feel

Good ◯
Tired ◯
Sore ◯
fatigued ◯

Goal Complete?

Yes ◯   No ◯

Notes

....
....
....
....
....
....
....
....
....

....
....
....
....

Date _____

Training distance _____

Time run _____

Location _____

Who you ran with _____

weather _____

How did you feel

Good ◯
Tired ◯
Sore ◯
fatigued ◯

Goal CompleteD?

Yes ◯   No ◯

Notes

....
....
....
....
....
....
....
....
....

....
....
....
....

Date _____

Training distance _____

Time run _____

Location _____

Who you ran with _____

weather _____

How did you feel

Good ◯
Tired ◯
Sore ◯
fatigued ◯

Goal Complete?

Yes ◯   No ◯

Notes

....
....
....
....
....
....
....
....

....
....
....
....

Date _____

Training distance _____

Time run _____

Location _____

Who you ran with _____

weather _____

How did you feel

Good ◯
Tired ◯
Sore ◯
fatigued ◯

Goal CompleteD?

Yes ◯   No ◯

Notes

....
....
....
....
....
....
....
....

....
....
....
....

Date _____

Training distance _____

Time run _____

Location _____

Who you ran with _____

weather _____

How did you feel

Good ◯
Tired ◯
Sore ◯
fatigued ◯

Goal Complete?

Yes ◯   No ◯

Notes

....
....
....
....
....
....
....
....

....
....
....
....

Date _____

Training distance _____

Time run _____

Location _____

Who you ran with _____

weather _____

How did you feel

Good ◯
Tired ◯
Sore ◯
fatigued ◯

Goal CompleteD?

Yes ◯   No ◯

Notes

....
....
....
....
....
....
....
....

....
....
....
....

Date

Training distance

Time run

Location

Who you ran with

weather

How did you feel

Goal Complete?

Yes ◯ No ◯

Good ◯
Tired ◯
Sore ◯
fatigued ◯

Notes

Date

Training distance

Time run

Location

Who you ran with

weather

How did you feel

Goal CompleteD?

Yes ◯ No ◯

Good ◯
Tired ◯
Sore ◯
fatigued ◯

Notes

Date

Training distance

Time run

Location

Who you ran with

weather

How did you feel

Good ○
Tired ○
Sore ○
fatigued ○

Goal Complete?

Yes ○   No ○

Notes

....
....
....
....
....
....
....

....
....
....
....

Date

Training distance

Time run

Location

Who you ran with

weather

How did you feel

Good ○
Tired ○
Sore ○
fatigued ○

Goal CompleteD?

Yes ○   No ○

Notes

....
....
....
....
....
....
....

....
....
....
....

Date _____

Training distance _____

Time run _____

Location _____

Who you ran with _____

weather _____

How did you feel

Goal Complete?

Yes ◯   No ◯

Good ◯
Tired ◯
Sore ◯
fatigued ◯

Notes

....
....
....
....
....
....
....

....
....
....
....
....

Date _____

Training distance _____

Time run _____

Location _____

Who you ran with _____

weather _____

How did you feel

Goal CompleteD?

Yes ◯   No ◯

Good ◯
Tired ◯
Sore ◯
fatigued ◯

Notes

....
....
....
....
....
....
....

....
....
....
....
....

Date _____

Training distance _____

Time run _____

Location _____

Who you ran with _____

weather _____

How did you feel

Good ○
Tired ○
Sore ○
fatigued ○

Goal Complete?

Yes ○   No ○

Notes

....
....
....
....
....
....
....
....

....
....
....

Date _____

Training distance _____

Time run _____

Location _____

Who you ran with _____

weather _____

How did you feel

Good ○
Tired ○
Sore ○
fatigued ○

Goal Completed?

Yes ○   No ○

Notes

....
....
....
....
....
....
....
....

....
....
....

Date _____

Training distance _____

Time run _____

Location _____

Who you ran with _____

weather _____

How did you feel

Good ◯
Tired ◯
Sore ◯
fatigued ◯

Goal Complete?

Yes ◯   No ◯

Notes

....
....
....
....
....
....
....

....
....
....
....

Date _____

Training distance _____

Time run _____

Location _____

Who you ran with _____

weather _____

How did you feel

Good ◯
Tired ◯
Sore ◯
fatigued ◯

Goal CompleteD?

Yes ◯   No ◯

Notes

....
....
....
....
....
....
....

....
....
....
....

Date _____

Training distance _____

Time run _____

Location _____

Who you ran with _____

weather _____

How did you feel

Goal Complete?

Yes ○   No ○

Good ○
Tired ○
Sore ○
fatigued ○

Notes

....
....
....
....
....
....
....
....
....

....
....
....
....

Date _____

Training distance _____

Time run _____

Location _____

Who you ran with _____

weather _____

How did you feel

Goal CompleteD?

Yes ○   No ○

Good ○
Tired ○
Sore ○
fatigued ○

Notes

....
....
....
....
....
....
....
....

....
....
....
....

Date _____

Training distance _____

Time run _____

Location _____

Who you ran with _____

weather _____

How did you feel

Goal Complete?

Yes ◯   No ◯

Good ◯
Tired ◯
Sore ◯
fatigued ◯

Notes

....
....
....
....
....
....
....
....
....
....
....
....

....
....
....
....

Date _____

Training distance _____

Time run _____

Location _____

Who you ran with _____

weather _____

How did you feel

Goal CompleteD?

Yes ◯   No ◯

Good ◯
Tired ◯
Sore ◯
fatigued ◯

Notes

....
....
....
....
....
....
....
....
....
....

....
....
....
....

Date _____

Training distance _____

Time run _____

Location _____

Who you ran with _____

weather _____

How did you feel

Good ◯
Tired ◯
Sore ◯
fatigued ◯

Goal Complete?

Yes ◯   No ◯

Notes
....
....
....
....
....
....
....
....
....

....
....
....

Date _____

Training distance _____

Time run _____

Location _____

Who you ran with _____

weather _____

How did you feel

Good ◯
Tired ◯
Sore ◯
fatigued ◯

Goal CompleteD?

Yes ◯   No ◯

Notes
....
....
....
....
....
....
....
....
....

....
....
....

Date _____

Training distance _____

Time run _____

Location _____

Who you ran with _____

weather _____

How did you feel

Good ◯
Tired ◯
Sore ◯
fatigued ◯

Goal Complete?

Yes ◯   No ◯

Notes

....
....
....
....
....
....
....

....
....
....
....

Date _____

Training distance _____

Time run _____

Location _____

Who you ran with _____

weather _____

How did you feel

Good ◯
Tired ◯
Sore ◯
fatigued ◯

Goal CompleteD?

Yes ◯   No ◯

Notes

....
....
....
....
....
....
....

....
....
....
....

Date _____

Training distance _____

Time run _____

Location _____

Who you ran with _____

weather _____

How did you feel

Goal Complete?

Yes ○   No ○

Good ○
Tired ○
Sore ○
fatigued ○

Notes

....
....
....
....
....
....
....

....
....
....
....

Date _____

Training distance _____

Time run _____

Location _____

Who you ran with _____

weather _____

How did you feel

Goal CompleteD?

Yes ○   No ○

Good ○
Tired ○
Sore ○
fatigued ○

Notes

....
....
....
....
....
....
....

....
....
....
....

Date _____

Training distance _____

Time run _____

Location _____

Who you ran with _____

weather _____

How did you feel

Goal Complete?

Yes ◯   No ◯

Good ◯
Tired ◯
Sore ◯
fatigued ◯

Notes

Date _____

Training distance _____

Time run _____

Location _____

Who you ran with _____

weather _____

How did you feel

Goal CompleteD?

Yes ◯   No ◯

Good ◯
Tired ◯
Sore ◯
fatigued ◯

Notes

Date _____

Training distance _____

Time run _____

Location _____

Who you ran with _____

weather _____

How did you feel

Goal Complete?

Yes ◯   No ◯

Good ◯
Tired ◯
Sore ◯
fatigued ◯

Notes

....
....
....
....
....
....
....
....

....
....
....
....

Date _____

Training distance _____

Time run _____

Location _____

Who you ran with _____

weather _____

How did you feel

Goal CompleteD?

Yes ◯   No ◯

Good ◯
Tired ◯
Sore ◯
fatigued ◯

Notes

....
....
....
....
....
....
....
....

....
....
....
....

Date _____

Training distance _____

Time run _____

Location _____

Who you ran with _____

weather _____

How did you feel

Goal Complete?

Yes ○   No ○

Good ○
Tired ○
Sore ○
fatigued ○

Notes

....
....
....
....
....
....
....

....
....
....
....

Date _____

Training distance _____

Time run _____

Location _____

Who you ran with _____

weather _____

How did you feel

Goal CompleteD?

Yes ○   No ○

Good ○
Tired ○
Sore ○
fatigued ○

Notes

....
....
....
....
....
....
....

....
....
....
....

Date _____

Training distance _____

Time run _____

Location _____

Who you ran with _____

weather _____

How did you feel

Goal Complete?

Yes ◯   No ◯

Good ◯
Tired ◯
Sore ◯
fatigued ◯

Notes

....
....
....
....
....
....
....
....

....
....
....
....

Date _____

Training distance _____

Time run _____

Location _____

Who you ran with _____

weather _____

How did you feel

Goal CompleteD?

Yes ◯   No ◯

Good ◯
Tired ◯
Sore ◯
fatigued ◯

Notes

....
....
....
....
....
....
....
....

....
....
....
....

Date _____

Training distance _____

Time run _____

Location _____

Who you ran with _____

weather _____

How did you feel   Good ○

Goal Complete?   Tired ○

Yes ○   No ○   Sore ○

fatigued ○

Notes

....
....
....
....
....
....
....

....
....
....
....

Date _____

Training distance _____

Time run _____

Location _____

Who you ran with _____

weather _____

How did you feel   Good ○

Goal CompleteD?   Tired ○

Yes ○   No ○   Sore ○

fatigued ○

Notes

....
....
....
....
....
....
....

....
....
....
....

Date _____

Training distance _____

Time run _____

Location _____

Who you ran with _____

weather _____

How did you feel

Good ◯
Tired ◯
Sore ◯
fatigued ◯

Goal Complete?

Yes ◯   No ◯

Notes

....
....
....
....
....
....
....
....

....
....
....
....

Date _____

Training distance _____

Time run _____

Location _____

Who you ran with _____

weather _____

How did you feel

Good ◯
Tired ◯
Sore ◯
fatigued ◯

Goal CompleteD?

Yes ◯   No ◯

Notes

....
....
....
....
....
....
....
....

....
....
....
....

Date _____

Training distance _____

Time run _____

Location _____

Who you ran with _____

weather _____

How did you feel

Good ◯

Tired ◯

Sore ◯

Goal Complete?

fatigued ◯

Yes ◯   No ◯

Notes

....
....
....
....
....
....
....
....
....

....
....
....
....

Date _____

Training distance _____

Time run _____

Location _____

Who you ran with _____

weather _____

How did you feel

Good ◯

Tired ◯

Sore ◯

Goal CompleteD?

fatigued ◯

Yes ◯   No ◯

Notes

....
....
....
....
....
....
....
....
....

....
....
....
....

Date

Training distance

Time run

Location

Who you ran with

weather

How did you feel

Goal Complete?

Yes ◯   No ◯

Good ◯
Tired ◯
Sore ◯
fatigued ◯

Notes

Date

Training distance

Time run

Location

Who you ran with

weather

How did you feel

Goal CompleteD?

Yes ◯   No ◯

Good ◯
Tired ◯
Sore ◯
fatigued ◯

Notes

Date

Training distance

Time run

Location

Who you ran with

weather

How did you feel

Goal Complete?

Yes ◯   No ◯

Good ◯
Tired ◯
Sore ◯
fatigued ◯

Notes

Date

Training distance

Time run

Location

Who you ran with

weather

How did you feel

Goal CompleteD?

Yes ◯   No ◯

Good ◯
Tired ◯
Sore ◯
fatigued ◯

Notes

Date _____

Training distance _____

Time run _____

Location _____

Who you ran with _____

weather _____

How did you feel

Goal Complete?

Yes ○   No ○

Good ○
Tired ○
Sore ○
fatigued ○

Notes

....
....
....
....
....
....
....
....

....
....
....

Date _____

Training distance _____

Time run _____

Location _____

Who you ran with _____

weather _____

How did you feel

Goal CompleteD?

Yes ○   No ○

Good ○
Tired ○
Sore ○
fatigued ○

Notes

....
....
....
....
....
....
....
....

....
....
....

Date

Training distance

Time run

Location

Who you ran with

weather

How did you feel

Good ○
Tired ○
Sore ○
fatigued ○

Goal Complete?

Yes ○   No ○

Notes

Date

Training distance

Time run

Location

Who you ran with

weather

How did you feel

Good ○
Tired ○
Sore ○
fatigued ○

Goal CompleteD?

Yes ○   No ○

Notes

Date _____

Training distance _____

Time run _____

Location _____

Who you ran with _____

weather _____

How did you feel   Good ◯

Goal Complete?   Tired ◯

Yes ◯   No ◯   Sore ◯

fatigued ◯

Notes

....
....
....
....
....
....
....
....

....
....
....

Date _____

Training distance _____

Time run _____

Location _____

Who you ran with _____

weather _____

How did you feel   Good ◯

Goal CompleteD?   Tired ◯

Yes ◯   No ◯   Sore ◯

fatigued ◯

Notes

....
....
....
....
....
....
....
....

....
....
....

Date

Training distance

Time run

Location

Who you ran with

weather

How did you feel

Goal Complete?

Yes ◯   No ◯

Good ◯
Tired ◯
Sore ◯
fatigued ◯

Notes

Date

Training distance

Time run

Location

Who you ran with

weather

How did you feel

Goal CompleteD?

Yes ◯   No ◯

Good ◯
Tired ◯
Sore ◯
fatigued ◯

Notes

Date _____

Training distance _____

Time run _____

Location _____

Who you ran with _____

weather _____

How did you feel
Good ◯
Tired ◯
Goal Complete?
Sore ◯
Yes ◯ No ◯
fatigued ◯

Notes
....
....
....
....
....
....
....
....
....
....

....
....
....
....

Date _____

Training distance _____

Time run _____

Location _____

Who you ran with _____

weather _____

How did you feel
Good ◯
Tired ◯
Goal CompleteD?
Sore ◯
Yes ◯ No ◯
fatigued ◯

Notes
....
....
....
....
....
....
....
....
....
....

....
....
....
....

Date _____

Training distance _____

Time run _____

Location _____

Who you ran with _____

weather _____

How did you feel

Good ◯
Tired ◯
Sore ◯
fatigued ◯

Goal Complete?

Yes ◯   No ◯

Notes

....
....
....
....
....
....
....
....

....
....
....
....

Date _____

Training distance _____

Time run _____

Location _____

Who you ran with _____

weather _____

How did you feel

Good ◯
Tired ◯
Sore ◯
fatigued ◯

Goal CompleteD?

Yes ◯   No ◯

Notes

....
....
....
....
....
....
....
....

....
....
....
....

Date _____

Training distance _____

Time run _____

Location _____

Who you ran with _____

weather _____

How did you feel

Goal Complete?

Yes ◯   No ◯

Good ◯
Tired ◯
Sore ◯
fatigued ◯

Notes

....
....
....
....
....
....
....
....
....
....

....
....
....
....

Date _____

Training distance _____

Time run _____

Location _____

Who you ran with _____

weather _____

How did you feel

Goal CompleteD?

Yes ◯   No ◯

Good ◯
Tired ◯
Sore ◯
fatigued ◯

Notes

....
....
....
....
....
....
....
....
....
....

....
....
....
....

Date _____

Training distance _____

Time run _____

Location _____

Who you ran with _____

weather _____

How did you feel

Good ◯
Tired ◯
Sore ◯
fatigued ◯

Goal Complete?

Yes ◯   No ◯

Notes

....
....
....
....
....
....
....
....
....

....
....
....
....

Date _____

Training distance _____

Time run _____

Location _____

Who you ran with _____

weather _____

How did you feel

Good ◯
Tired ◯
Sore ◯
fatigued ◯

Goal CompleteD?

Yes ◯   No ◯

Notes

....
....
....
....
....
....
....
....
....

....
....
....
....

Date _____

Training distance _____

Time run _____

Location _____

Who you ran with _____

weather _____

How did you feel Good ◯ Tired ◯ Sore ◯ fatigued ◯

Goal Complete?

Yes ◯   No ◯

Notes

....
....
....
....
....
....
....
....

....
....
....

Date _____

Training distance _____

Time run _____

Location _____

Who you ran with _____

weather _____

How did you feel Good ◯ Tired ◯ Sore ◯ fatigued ◯

Goal CompleteD?

Yes ◯   No ◯

Notes

....
....
....
....
....
....
....

....
....
....

Date

Training distance

Time run

Location

Who you ran with

weather

How did you feel

Good ⃝
Tired ⃝
Sore ⃝
fatigued ⃝

Goal Complete?

Yes ⃝   No ⃝

Notes

Date

Training distance

Time run

Location

Who you ran with

weather

How did you feel

Good ⃝
Tired ⃝
Sore ⃝
fatigued ⃝

Goal CompleteD?

Yes ⃝   No ⃝

Notes

Date _____

Training distance _____

Time run _____

Location _____

Who you ran with _____

weather _____

How did you feel
Good ◯
Tired ◯
Sore ◯

Goal Complete?
Yes ◯ No ◯
fatigued ◯

Notes
....
....
....
....
....
....

....
....
....
....

Date _____

Training distance _____

Time run _____

Location _____

Who you ran with _____

weather _____

How did you feel
Good ◯
Tired ◯
Sore ◯

Goal CompleteD?
Yes ◯ No ◯
fatigued ◯

Notes
....
....
....
....
....
....

....
....
....

Date
_____

Training distance
_____

Time run
_____

Location
_____

Who you ran with
_____

weather
_____

How did you feel

Good ⃝
Tired ⃝
Sore ⃝
fatigued ⃝

Goal Complete?

Yes ⃝   No ⃝

Notes

....
....
....
....
....
....
....
....
....

....
....
....
....

Date
_____

Training distance
_____

Time run
_____

Location
_____

Who you ran with
_____

weather

How did you feel

Good ⃝
Tired ⃝
Sore ⃝
fatigued ⃝

Goal CompleteD?

Yes ⃝   No ⃝

Notes

....
....
....
....
....
....
....
....

....
....
....
....

Date
_____

Training distance
_____

Time run
_____

Location
_____

Who you ran with
_____

weather
_____

How did you feel

Good ◯
Tired ◯
Sore ◯
fatigued ◯

Goal Complete?

Yes ◯   No ◯

Notes

....
....
....
....
....
....
....
....
....
....
....

....
....
....
....

Date
_____

Training distance
_____

Time run
_____

Location
_____

Who you ran with
_____

weather
_____

How did you feel

Good ◯
Tired ◯
Sore ◯
fatigued ◯

Goal CompleteD?

Yes ◯   No ◯

Notes

....
....
....
....
....
....
....
....
....
....
....

....
....
....
....

Date

Training distance

Time run

Location

Who you ran with

weather

How did you feel

Goal Complete?

Yes ◯   No ◯

Good ◯
Tired ◯
Sore ◯
fatigued ◯

Notes

Date

Training distance

Time run

Location

Who you ran with

weather

How did you feel

Goal CompleteD?

Yes ◯   No ◯

Good ◯
Tired ◯
Sore ◯
fatigued ◯

Notes

Date

Training distance

Time run

Location

Who you ran with

weather

How did you feel

Goal Complete?

Yes ◯ No ◯

Good ◯
Tired ◯
Sore ◯
fatigued ◯

Notes

Date

Training distance

Time run

Location

Who you ran with

weather

How did you feel

Goal CompleteD?

Yes ◯ No ◯

Good ◯
Tired ◯
Sore ◯
fatigued ◯

Notes

Date _____

Training distance _____

Time run _____

Location _____

Who you ran with _____

weather _____

How did you feel

Goal Complete?

Yes ◯   No ◯

Good ◯
Tired ◯
Sore ◯
fatigued ◯

Notes

....
....
....
....
....
....
....

....
....
....

Date _____

Training distance _____

Time run _____

Location _____

Who you ran with _____

weather _____

How did you feel

Goal CompleteD?

Yes ◯   No ◯

Good ◯
Tired ◯
Sore ◯
fatigued ◯

Notes

....
....
....
....
....
....

....
....
....

Date _____

Training distance _____

Time run _____

Location _____

Who you ran with _____

weather _____

How did you feel

Goal Complete?

Yes ◯ No ◯

Good ◯
Tired ◯
Sore ◯
fatigued ◯

Notes

. . . .
. . . .
. . . .
. . . .
. . . .
. . . .
. . . .

. . . .
. . . .
. . . .
. . . .

Date _____

Training distance _____

Time run _____

Location _____

Who you ran with _____

weather _____

How did you feel

Goal CompleteD?

Yes ◯ No ◯

Good ◯
Tired ◯
Sore ◯
fatigued ◯

Notes

. . . .
. . . .
. . . .
. . . .
. . . .
. . . .

. . . .
. . . .
. . . .

Date _____

Training distance _____

Time run _____

Location _____

Who you ran with _____

weather _____

How did you feel

Goal Complete?

Yes ◯   No ◯

Good ◯
Tired ◯
Sore ◯
fatigued ◯

Notes

....
....
....
....
....
....
....
....
....

....
....
....
....

Date _____

Training distance _____

Time run _____

Location _____

Who you ran with _____

weather _____

How did you feel

Goal CompleteD?

Yes ◯   No ◯

Good ◯
Tired ◯
Sore ◯
fatigued ◯

Notes

....
....
....
....
....
....
....
....
....

....
....
....
....

Date _____

Training distance _____

Time run _____

Location _____

Who you ran with _____

weather _____

How did you feel

Goal Complete?

Yes ◯   No ◯

Good ◯
Tired ◯
Sore ◯
fatigued ◯

Notes

....
....
....
....
....
....
....
....
....
....

....
....
....
....

Date _____

Training distance _____

Time run _____

Location _____

Who you ran with _____

weather _____

How did you feel

Goal CompleteD?

Yes ◯   No ◯

Good ◯
Tired ◯
Sore ◯
fatigued ◯

Notes

....
....
....
....
....
....
....
....
....
....

....
....
....
....

Date

Training distance

Time run

Location

Who you ran with

weather

How did you feel

Goal Complete?

Yes ◯   No ◯

Good ◯
Tired ◯
Sore ◯
fatigued ◯

Notes

Date

Training distance

Time run

Location

Who you ran with

weather

How did you feel

Goal CompleteD?

Yes ◯   No ◯

Good ◯
Tired ◯
Sore ◯
fatigued ◯

Notes

Date _____

Training distance _____

Time run _____

Location _____

Who you ran with _____

weather _____

How did you feel

Goal Complete?

Yes ◯   No ◯

Good ◯
Tired ◯
Sore ◯
fatigued ◯

Notes
....
....
....
....
....
....
....
....
....

....
....
....

Date _____

Training distance _____

Time run _____

Location _____

Who you ran with _____

weather _____

How did you feel

Goal CompleteD?

Yes ◯   No ◯

Good ◯
Tired ◯
Sore ◯
fatigued ◯

Notes
....
....
....
....
....
....
....
....
....

....
....
....

Date _____

Training distance _____

Time run _____

Location _____

Who you ran with _____

weather _____

How did you feel

Goal Complete?

Yes ◯   No ◯

Good ◯
Tired ◯
Sore ◯
fatigued ◯

Notes

....
....
....
....
....
....
....
....
....
....
....
....

....
....
....
....

Date _____

Training distance _____

Time run _____

Location _____

Who you ran with _____

weather _____

How did you feel

Goal CompleteD?

Yes ◯   No ◯

Good ◯
Tired ◯
Sore ◯
fatigued ◯

Notes

....
....
....
....
....
....
....
....
....
....

....
....
....
....

Date _____

Training distance _____

Time run _____

Location _____

Who you ran with _____

weather _____

How did you feel

Good ◯
Tired ◯
Sore ◯
fatigued ◯

Goal Complete?

Yes ◯   No ◯

Notes
....
....
....
....
....
....
....

....
....
....
....

Date _____

Training distance _____

Time run _____

Location _____

Who you ran with _____

weather _____

How did you feel

Good ◯
Tired ◯
Sore ◯
fatigued ◯

Goal CompleteD?

Yes ◯   No ◯

Notes
....
....
....
....
....
....
....

....
....
....
....

Date _____

Training distance _____

Time run _____

Location _____

Who you ran with _____

weather _____

How did you feel   Good ◯
                        Tired ◯
Goal Complete?   Sore ◯
Yes ◯   No ◯   fatigued ◯

Notes

....
....
....
....
....
....
....

....
....
....
....

Date _____

Training distance _____

Time run _____

Location _____

Who you ran with _____

weather _____

How did you feel   Good ◯
                        Tired ◯
Goal CompleteD?   Sore ◯
Yes ◯   No ◯   fatigued ◯

Notes

....
....
....
....
....
....
....

....
....
....
....

Date

Training distance

Time run

Location

Who you ran with

weather

How did you feel

Goal Complete?

Yes ◯   No ◯

Good ◯
Tired ◯
Sore ◯
fatigued ◯

Notes
....
....
....
....
....
....
....

....
....
....

Date

Training distance

Time run

Location

Who you ran with

weather

How did you feel

Goal CompleteD?

Yes ◯   No ◯

Good ◯
Tired ◯
Sore ◯
fatigued ◯

Notes
....
....
....
....
....
....
....

....
....
....

Date _____

Training distance _____

Time run _____

Location _____

Who you ran with _____

weather _____

How did you feel

Goal Complete?

Yes ⃝   No ⃝

Good ⃝
Tired ⃝
Sore ⃝
fatigued ⃝

Notes

....
....
....
....
....
....
....
....

....
....
....
....

Date _____

Training distance _____

Time run _____

Location _____

Who you ran with _____

weather _____

How did you feel

Goal CompleteD?

Yes ⃝   No ⃝

Good ⃝
Tired ⃝
Sore ⃝
fatigued ⃝

Notes

....
....
....
....
....
....
....
....

....
....
....
....

Date

Training distance

Time run

Location

Who you ran with

weather

How did you feel

Goal Complete?

Yes ◯   No ◯

Good ◯
Tired ◯
Sore ◯
fatigued ◯

Notes

Date

Training distance

Time run

Location

Who you ran with

weather

How did you feel

Goal CompleteD?

Yes ◯   No ◯

Good ◯
Tired ◯
Sore ◯
fatigued ◯

Notes

Date

Training distance

Time run

Location

Who you ran with

weather

How did you feel

Good ◯
Tired ◯
Sore ◯

Goal Complete?

Yes ◯   No ◯

fatigued ◯

Notes

Date

Training distance

Time run

Location

Who you ran with

weather

How did you feel

Good ◯
Tired ◯
Sore ◯

Goal CompleteD?

Yes ◯   No ◯

fatigued ◯

Notes

Date ....

Training distance ....

Time run ....

Location ....

Who you ran with ....

weather ....

How did you feel

Goal Complete?

Yes ◯   No ◯

Good ◯
Tired ◯
Sore ◯
fatigued ◯

Notes

....
....
....
....
....
....
....
....
....

....
....
....
....

Date ....

Training distance ....

Time run ....

Location ....

Who you ran with ....

weather ....

How did you feel

Goal CompleteD?

Yes ◯   No ◯

Good ◯
Tired ◯
Sore ◯
fatigued ◯

Notes

....
....
....
....
....
....
....
....
....

....
....
....
....

Date _____

Training distance _____

Time run _____

Location _____

Who you ran with _____

weather _____

How did you feel

Goal Complete?

Yes ○ No ○

Good ○
Tired ○
Sore ○
fatigued ○

Notes

....
....
....
....
....
....
....
....

....
....
....

Date _____

Training distance _____

Time run _____

Location _____

Who you ran with _____

weather _____

How did you feel

Goal CompleteD?

Yes ○ No ○

Good ○
Tired ○
Sore ○
fatigued ○

Notes

....
....
....
....
....
....
....
....

....
....
....
....

Date _____

Training distance _____

Time run _____

Location _____

Who you ran with _____

weather _____

How did you feel

Good ◯
Tired ◯
Sore ◯
fatigued ◯

Goal Complete?

Yes ◯   No ◯

Notes

....
....
....
....
....
....
....
....

....
....
....
....

Date _____

Training distance _____

Time run _____

Location _____

Who you ran with _____

weather _____

How did you feel

Good ◯
Tired ◯
Sore ◯
fatigued ◯

Goal CompleteD?

Yes ◯   No ◯

Notes

....
....
....
....
....
....
....
....

....
....
....
....

Date _____

Training distance _____

Time run _____

Location _____

Who you ran with _____

weather _____

How did you feel

Goal Complete?

Yes ◯   No ◯

Good ◯
Tired ◯
Sore ◯
fatigued ◯

Notes

....
....
....
....
....
....
....

....
....
....
....

Date _____

Training distance _____

Time run _____

Location _____

Who you ran with _____

weather _____

How did you feel

Goal CompleteD?

Yes ◯   No ◯

Good ◯
Tired ◯
Sore ◯
fatigued ◯

Notes

....
....
....
....
....
....
....

....
....
....
....

Date

Training distance

Time run

Location

Who you ran with

weather

How did you feel

Good ◯
Tired ◯
Sore ◯
fatigued ◯

Goal Complete?

Yes ◯ No ◯

Notes

Date

Training distance

Time run

Location

Who you ran with

weather

How did you feel

Good ◯
Tired ◯
Sore ◯
fatigued ◯

Goal CompleteD?

Yes ◯ No ◯

Notes

Date

Training distance

Time run

Location

Who you ran with

weather

How did you feel

Goal Complete?

Yes ◯ No ◯

Good ◯
Tired ◯
Sore ◯
fatigued ◯

Notes

Date

Training distance

Time run

Location

Who you ran with

weather

How did you feel

Goal CompleteD?

Yes ◯ No ◯

Good ◯
Tired ◯
Sore ◯
fatigued ◯

Notes

Date _____

Training distance _____

Time run _____

Location _____

Who you ran with _____

weather _____

How did you feel

Goal Complete?

Yes ◯ No ◯

Good ◯
Tired ◯
Sore ◯
fatigued ◯

Notes

....
....
....
....
....
....
....
....
....
....

....
....
....
....

Date _____

Training distance _____

Time run _____

Location _____

Who you ran with _____

weather _____

How did you feel

Goal CompleteD?

Yes ◯ No ◯

Good ◯
Tired ◯
Sore ◯
fatigued ◯

Notes

....
....
....
....
....
....
....
....
....
....

....
....
....

Date _____

Training distance _____

Time run _____

Location _____

Who you ran with _____

weather _____

How did you feel

Good ○
Tired ○
Sore ○
fatigued ○

Goal Complete?

Yes ○   No ○

Notes

....
....
....
....
....
....
....
....

....
....
....
....

Date _____

Training distance _____

Time run _____

Location _____

Who you ran with _____

weather _____

How did you feel

Good ○
Tired ○
Sore ○
fatigued ○

Goal CompleteD?

Yes ○   No ○

Notes

....
....
....
....
....
....
....
....

....
....
....
....

Entry 1

Date _____

Training distance _____

Time run _____

Location _____

Who you ran with _____

weather _____

How did you feel
- Good ◯
- Tired ◯
- Sore ◯
- fatigued ◯

Goal Complete?

Yes ◯ No ◯

Notes

....
....
....
....
....
....
....
....

....
....
....
....

Entry 2

Date _____

Training distance _____

Time run _____

Location _____

Who you ran with _____

weather _____

How did you feel
- Good ◯
- Tired ◯
- Sore ◯
- fatigued ◯

Goal CompleteD?

Yes ◯ No ◯

Notes

....
....
....
....
....
....
....
....

....
....
....
....

Date _____

Training distance _____

Time run _____

Location _____

Who you ran with _____

weather _____

How did you feel

Goal Complete?

Yes ◯   No ◯

Good ◯
Tired ◯
Sore ◯
fatigued ◯

Notes

....
....
....
....
....
....
....
....

....
....
....
....

Date _____

Training distance _____

Time run _____

Location _____

Who you ran with _____

weather _____

How did you feel

Goal CompleteD?

Yes ◯   No ◯

Good ◯
Tired ◯
Sore ◯
fatigued ◯

Notes

....
....
....
....
....

....
....
....
....

Date _____

Training distance _____

Time run _____

Location _____

Who you ran with _____

weather _____

How did you feel
Good ◯
Tired ◯
Sore ◯

Goal Complete?
Yes ◯ No ◯
fatigued ◯

Notes
....
....
....
....
....
....
....
....
....

....
....
....
....

Date _____

Training distance _____

Time run _____

Location _____

Who you ran with _____

weather _____

How did you feel
Good ◯
Tired ◯
Sore ◯

Goal CompleteD?
Yes ◯ No ◯
fatigued ◯

Notes
....
....
....
....
....
....
....
....
....

....
....
....
....

Date _____

Training distance _____

Time run _____

Location _____

Who you ran with _____

weather _____

How did you feel

Goal Complete?

Yes ○   No ○

Good ○
Tired ○
Sore ○
fatigued ○

Notes

....
....
....
....
....
....
....
....
....

Date _____

Training distance _____

Time run _____

Location _____

Who you ran with _____

weather _____

How did you feel

Goal CompleteD?

Yes ○   No ○

Good ○
Tired ○
Sore ○
fatigued ○

Notes

....
....
....
....
....
....
....
....
....

Date

Training distance

Time run

Location

Who you ran with

weather

How did you feel

Goal Complete?

Yes ◯   No ◯

Good ◯
Tired ◯
Sore ◯
fatigued ◯

Notes

....
....
....
....
....
....
....
....

....
....
....

Date

Training distance

Time run

Location

Who you ran with

weather

How did you feel

Goal CompleteD?

Yes ◯   No ◯

Good ◯
Tired ◯
Sore ◯
fatigued ◯

Notes

....
....
....
....
....
....
....
....

....
....
....

Date _____

Training distance _____

Time run _____

Location _____

Who you ran with _____

weather _____

How did you feel

Goal Complete?

Yes ○   No ○

Good ○
Tired ○
Sore ○
fatigued ○

Notes

....
....
....
....
....
....
....
....
....

....
....
....
....

Date _____

Training distance _____

Time run _____

Location _____

Who you ran with _____

weather _____

How did you feel

Goal CompleteD?

Yes ○   No ○

Good ○
Tired ○
Sore ○
fatigued ○

Notes

....
....
....
....
....
....
....
....
....

....
....
....
....

Date _____

Training distance _____

Time run _____

Location _____

Who you ran with _____

weather _____

How did you feel

Goal Complete?

Yes ◯   No ◯

Good ◯
Tired ◯
Sore ◯
fatigued ◯

Notes

Date _____

Training distance _____

Time run _____

Location _____

Who you ran with _____

weather _____

How did you feel

Goal CompleteD?

Yes ◯   No ◯

Good ◯
Tired ◯
Sore ◯
fatigued ◯

Notes

Date

Training distance

Time run

Location

Who you ran with

weather

How did you feel

Goal Complete?

Yes ◯   No ◯

Good ◯
Tired ◯
Sore ◯
fatigued ◯

Notes

Date

Training distance

Time run

Location

Who you ran with

weather

How did you feel

Goal CompleteD?

Yes ◯   No ◯

Good ◯
Tired ◯
Sore ◯
fatigued ◯

Notes

Date

Training distance

Time run

Location

Who you ran with

weather

How did you feel

Goal Complete?

Yes ◯   No ◯

Good ◯
Tired ◯
Sore ◯
fatigued ◯

Notes

Date

Training distance

Time run

Location

Who you ran with

weather

How did you feel

Goal CompleteD?

Yes ◯   No ◯

Good ◯
Tired ◯
Sore ◯
fatigued ◯

Notes

Date _____

Training distance _____

Time run _____

Location _____

Who you ran with _____

weather _____

How did you feel

Good ○
Tired ○
Sore ○
fatigued ○

Goal Complete?

Yes ○   No ○

Notes

....
....
....
....
....
....
....
....
....

....
....
....
....

Date _____

Training distance _____

Time run _____

Location _____

Who you ran with _____

weather _____

How did you feel

Good ○
Tired ○
Sore ○
fatigued ○

Goal CompleteD?

Yes ○   No ○

Notes

....
....
....
....
....
....
....
....
....

....
....
....
....

Date

Training distance

Time run

Location

Who you ran with

weather

How did you feel

Good ◯
Tired ◯
Sore ◯
fatigued ◯

Goal Complete?

Yes ◯   No ◯

Notes

Date

Training distance

Time run

Location

Who you ran with

weather

How did you feel

Good ◯
Tired ◯
Sore ◯
fatigued ◯

Goal CompleteD?

Yes ◯   No ◯

Notes

Date _____

Training distance _____

Time run _____

Location _____

Who you ran with _____

weather _____

How did you feel

Goal Complete?

Yes ◯   No ◯

Good ◯
Tired ◯
Sore ◯
fatigued ◯

Notes

Date _____

Training distance _____

Time run _____

Location _____

Who you ran with _____

weather _____

How did you feel

Goal CompleteD?

Yes ◯   No ◯

Good ◯
Tired ◯
Sore ◯
fatigued ◯

Notes

Date _____

Training distance _____

Time run _____

Location _____

Who you ran with _____

weather _____

How did you feel

Good ◯
Tired ◯
Sore ◯
fatigued ◯

Goal Complete?

Yes ◯   No ◯

Notes

....
....
....
....
....
....
....
....
....
....
....

....
....
....

Date _____

Training distance _____

Time run _____

Location _____

Who you ran with _____

weather _____

How did you feel

Good ◯
Tired ◯
Sore ◯
fatigued ◯

Goal CompleteD?

Yes ◯   No ◯

Notes

....
....
....
....
....
....
....
....
....
....
....

....
....
....

Date _____

Training distance _____

Time run _____

Location _____

Who you ran with _____

weather _____

How did you feel

Good ◯
Tired ◯
Sore ◯
fatigued ◯

Goal Complete?

Yes ◯   No ◯

Notes

....
....
....
....
....
....
....
....
....
....

....
....
....
....

Date _____

Training distance _____

Time run _____

Location _____

Who you ran with _____

weather _____

How did you feel

Good ◯
Tired ◯
Sore ◯
fatigued ◯

Goal CompleteD?

Yes ◯   No ◯

Notes

....
....
....
....
....
....
....
....
....
....

....
....
....
....

Date

Training distance

Time run

Location

Who you ran with

weather

Notes

How did you feel

Good ◯
Tired ◯
Sore ◯
fatigued ◯

Goal Complete?

Yes ◯   No ◯

Date

Training distance

Time run

Location

Who you ran with

weather

Notes

How did you feel

Good ◯
Tired ◯
Sore ◯
fatigued ◯

Goal CompleteD?

Yes ◯   No ◯

Date _____

Training distance _____

Time run _____

Location _____

Who you ran with _____

weather _____

How did you feel

Good ◯
Tired ◯
Sore ◯
fatigued ◯

Goal Complete?

Yes ◯   No ◯

Notes

....
....
....
....
....
....
....
....
....
....

....
....
....
....

Date _____

Training distance _____

Time run _____

Location _____

Who you ran with _____

weather _____

How did you feel

Good ◯
Tired ◯
Sore ◯
fatigued ◯

Goal CompleteD?

Yes ◯   No ◯

Notes

....
....
....
....
....
....
....
....
....
....

....
....
....
....

Date

Training distance

Time run

Location

Who you ran with

weather

How did you feel

Good ◯
Tired ◯
Sore ◯
fatigued ◯

Goal Complete?

Yes ◯   No ◯

Notes

Date

Training distance

Time run

Location

Who you ran with

weather

How did you feel

Good ◯
Tired ◯
Sore ◯
fatigued ◯

Goal CompleteD?

Yes ◯   No ◯

Notes

Date _____

Training distance _____

Time run _____

Location _____

Who you ran with _____

weather _____

How did you feel

Good ○
Tired ○
Sore ○
fatigued ○

Goal Complete?

Yes ○   No ○

Notes

....
....
....
....
....
....
....
....
....
....
....

....
....
....
....

Date _____

Training distance _____

Time run _____

Location _____

Who you ran with _____

weather _____

How did you feel

Good ○
Tired ○
Sore ○
fatigued ○

Goal CompleteD?

Yes ○   No ○

Notes

....
....
....
....
....
....
....
....
....
....
....

....
....
....
....

Date _____

Training distance _____

Time run _____

Location _____

Who you ran with _____

weather _____

How did you feel   Good ◯

Goal Complete?   Tired ◯

Yes ◯   No ◯   Sore ◯

                     fatigued ◯

Notes

....
....
....
....
....
....
....
....

....
....
....
....

Date _____

Training distance _____

Time run _____

Location _____

Who you ran with _____

weather _____

How did you feel   Good ◯

Goal CompleteD?   Tired ◯

Yes ◯   No ◯   Sore ◯

                     fatigued ◯

Notes

....
....
....
....
....
....
....

....
....
....
....

Date _____

Training distance _____

Time run _____

Location _____

Who you ran with _____

weather _____

How did you feel

Goal Complete?

Yes ◯   No ◯

Good ◯
Tired ◯
Sore ◯
fatigued ◯

Notes

....
....
....
....
....
....
....
....

....
....
....
....

Date _____

Training distance _____

Time run _____

Location _____

Who you ran with _____

weather _____

How did you feel

Goal CompleteD?

Yes ◯   No ◯

Good ◯
Tired ◯
Sore ◯
fatigued ◯

Notes

....
....
....
....
....
....
....
....

....
....
....
....

Date

Training distance

Time run

Location

Who you ran with

weather

How did you feel

Goal Complete?

Yes ○   No ○

Good ○
Tired ○
Sore ○
fatigued ○

Notes

....
....
....
....
....
....
....
....
....

....
....
....

Date

Training distance

Time run

Location

Who you ran with

weather

How did you feel

Goal CompleteD?

Yes ○   No ○

Good ○
Tired ○
Sore ○
fatigued ○

Notes

....
....
....
....
....
....
....
....
....

....
....
....

Date

Training distance

Time run

Location

Who you ran with

weather

How did you feel

Goal Complete?

Yes ◯   No ◯

Good ◯
Tired ◯
Sore ◯
fatigued ◯

Notes

Date

Training distance

Time run

Location

Who you ran with

weather

How did you feel

Goal CompleteD?

Yes ◯   No ◯

Good ◯
Tired ◯
Sore ◯
fatigued ◯

Notes

Date

Training distance

Time run

Location

Who you ran with

weather

How did you feel

Goal Complete?

Yes ◯ No ◯

Good ◯
Tired ◯
Sore ◯
fatigued ◯

Notes

Date

Training distance

Time run

Location

Who you ran with

weather

How did you feel

Goal CompleteD?

Yes ◯ No ◯

Good ◯
Tired ◯
Sore ◯
fatigued ◯

Notes

Date _____

Training distance _____

Time run _____

Location _____

Who you ran with _____

weather _____

How did you feel Good ◯

Tired ◯

Goal Complete? Sore ◯

Yes ◯ No ◯ fatigued ◯

Notes

....
....
....
....
....
....
....
....
....

....
....
....
....

Date _____

Training distance _____

Time run _____

Location _____

Who you ran with _____

weather _____

How did you feel Good ◯

Tired ◯

Goal CompleteD? Sore ◯

Yes ◯ No ◯ fatigued ◯

Notes

....
....
....
....
....
....
....
....
....

....
....
....
....

Date

Training distance

Time run

Location

Who you ran with

weather

How did you feel

Goal Complete?

Yes ○   No ○

Good ○
Tired ○
Sore ○
fatigued ○

Notes

Date

Training distance

Time run

Location

Who you ran with

weather

How did you feel

Goal CompleteD?

Yes ○   No ○

Good ○
Tired ○
Sore ○
fatigued ○

Notes

Date _____

Training distance _____

Time run _____

Location _____

Who you ran with _____

weather _____

How did you feel

Goal Complete?

Yes ◯   No ◯

Good ◯
Tired ◯
Sore ◯
fatigued ◯

Notes

....
....
....
....
....
....
....
....
....
....
....

....
....
....
....

Date _____

Training distance _____

Time run _____

Location _____

Who you ran with _____

weather _____

How did you feel

Goal CompleteD?

Yes ◯   No ◯

Good ◯
Tired ◯
Sore ◯
fatigued ◯

Notes

....
....
....
....
....
....
....
....
....
....

....
....
....
....

Date _____

Training distance _____

Time run _____

Location _____

Who you ran with _____

weather _____

How did you feel   Good ◯

Goal Complete?   Tired ◯

Yes ◯   No ◯   Sore ◯

fatigued ◯

Notes

....
....
....
....
....
....
....
....
....

....
....
....
....

Date _____

Training distance _____

Time run _____

Location _____

Who you ran with _____

weather _____

How did you feel   Good ◯

Goal CompleteD?   Tired ◯

Yes ◯   No ◯   Sore ◯

fatigued ◯

Notes

....
....
....
....
....
....
....
....

....
....
....
....

Date _____

Training distance _____

Time run _____

Location _____

Who you ran with _____

weather _____

How did you feel

Goal Complete?

Yes ○   No ○

Good ○
Tired ○
Sore ○
fatigued ○

Notes

....
....
....
....
....
....
....
....
....

....
....
....
....

Date _____

Training distance _____

Time run _____

Location _____

Who you ran with _____

weather _____

How did you feel

Goal CompleteD?

Yes ○   No ○

Good ○
Tired ○
Sore ○
fatigued ○

Notes

....
....
....
....
....
....
....
....
....

....
....
....
....

Date

Training distance

Time run

Location

Who you ran with

weather

How did you feel

Goal Complete?

Yes ◯   No ◯

Good ◯
Tired ◯
Sore ◯
fatigued ◯

Notes

Date

Training distance

Time run

Location

Who you ran with

weather

How did you feel

Goal CompleteD?

Yes ◯   No ◯

Good ◯
Tired ◯
Sore ◯
fatigued ◯

Notes

Date _____

Training distance _____

Time run _____

Location _____

Who you ran with _____

weather _____

How did you feel   Good ◯

Goal Complete?   Tired ◯
                     Sore ◯
Yes ◯   No ◯   fatigued ◯

Notes
....
....
....
....
....
....
....
....

....
....
....
....

Date _____

Training distance _____

Time run _____

Location _____

Who you ran with _____

weather _____

How did you feel   Good ◯

Goal CompleteD?   Tired ◯
                     Sore ◯
Yes ◯   No ◯   fatigued ◯

Notes
....
....
....
....
....
....
....
....

....
....
....
....

Date _____

Training distance _____

Time run _____

Location _____

Who you ran with _____

weather _____

How did you feel   Good ○

Goal Complete?   Tired ○

Yes ○   No ○   Sore ○

fatigued ○

Notes

....
....
....
....
....
....
....
....
....
....
....

....
....
....

Date _____

Training distance _____

Time run _____

Location _____

Who you ran with _____

weather _____

How did you feel   Good ○

Goal CompleteD?   Tired ○

Yes ○   No ○   Sore ○

fatigued ○

Notes

....
....
....
....
....
....
....
....
....
....
....

....
....
....

Date _____

Training distance _____

Time run _____

Location _____

Who you ran with _____

weather _____

How did you feel

Goal Complete?

Yes ◯ No ◯

Good ◯
Tired ◯
Sore ◯
fatigued ◯

Notes

....
....
....
....
....
....
....
....
....
....

....
....
....
....

Date _____

Training distance _____

Time run _____

Location _____

Who you ran with _____

weather _____

How did you feel

Goal CompleteD?

Yes ◯ No ◯

Good ◯
Tired ◯
Sore ◯
fatigued ◯

Notes

....
....
....
....
....
....
....
....
....
....

....
....
....
....

Date _____

Training distance _____

Time run _____

Location _____

Who you ran with _____

weather _____

How did you feel   Good ◯

Goal Complete?   Tired ◯

Yes ◯   No ◯   Sore ◯

fatigued ◯

Notes

....
....
....
....
....
....
....
....

....
....
....
....

Date _____

Training distance _____

Time run _____

Location _____

Who you ran with _____

weather _____

How did you feel   Good ◯

Goal CompleteD?   Tired ◯

Yes ◯   No ◯   Sore ◯

fatigued ◯

Notes

....
....
....
....
....
....
....
....

....
....
....
....

Entry 1

Date _____

Training distance _____

Time run _____

Location _____

Who you ran with _____

weather _____

How did you feel

Good ◯
Tired ◯
Sore ◯
fatigued ◯

Goal Complete?

Yes ◯   No ◯

Notes

....
....
....
....
....
....
....
....

....
....
....
....

Entry 2

Date _____

Training distance _____

Time run _____

Location _____

Who you ran with _____

weather _____

How did you feel

Good ◯
Tired ◯
Sore ◯
fatigued ◯

Goal CompleteD?

Yes ◯   No ◯

Notes

....
....
....
....
....
....
....
....

....
....
....
....

Date

Training distance

Time run

Location

Who you ran with

weather

Notes

How did you feel

Good ◯
Tired ◯
Sore ◯
fatigued ◯

Goal Complete?

Yes ◯   No ◯

Date

Training distance

Time run

Location

Who you ran with

weather

Notes

How did you feel

Good ◯
Tired ◯
Sore ◯
fatigued ◯

Goal CompleteD?

Yes ◯   No ◯

Date _____

Training distance _____

Time run _____

Location _____

Who you ran with _____

weather _____

How did you feel

Goal Complete?

Yes ◯ No ◯

Good ◯
Tired ◯
Sore ◯
fatigued ◯

Notes

Date _____

Training distance _____

Time run _____

Location _____

Who you ran with _____

weather _____

How did you feel

Goal CompleteD?

Yes ◯ No ◯

Good ◯
Tired ◯
Sore ◯
fatigued ◯

Notes

Date

Training distance

Time run

Location

Who you ran with

weather

How did you feel

Goal Complete?

Yes ○   No ○

Good ○
Tired ○
Sore ○
fatigued ○

Notes

Date

Training distance

Time run

Location

Who you ran with

weather

How did you feel

Goal CompleteD?

Yes ○   No ○

Good ○
Tired ○
Sore ○
fatigued ○

Notes

Date _____

Training distance _____

Time run _____

Location _____

Who you ran with _____

weather _____

How did you feel

Goal Complete?

Yes ○   No ○

Good ○
Tired ○
Sore ○
fatigued ○

Notes

....
....
....
....
....
....
....
....
....
....
....

....
....
....
....

Date _____

Training distance _____

Time run _____

Location _____

Who you ran with _____

weather _____

How did you feel

Goal CompleteD?

Yes ○   No ○

Good ○
Tired ○
Sore ○
fatigued ○

Notes

....
....
....
....
....
....
....
....
....
....

....
....
....
....

Date _____

Training distance _____

Time run _____

Location _____

Who you ran with _____

weather _____

How did you feel Good ◯ Tired ◯

Goal Complete? Sore ◯ fatigued ◯

Yes ◯ No ◯

Notes

....
....
....
....
....
....
....

....
....
....

Date _____

Training distance _____

Time run _____

Location _____

Who you ran with _____

weather _____

How did you feel Good ◯ Tired ◯

Goal CompleteD? Sore ◯ fatigued ◯

Yes ◯ No ◯

Notes

....
....
....
....
....
....
....

....
....
....

Date _____

Training distance _____

Time run _____

Location _____

Who you ran with _____

weather _____

How did you feel

Goal Complete?

Yes ◯ No ◯

Good ◯
Tired ◯
Sore ◯
fatigued ◯

Notes

Date _____

Training distance _____

Time run _____

Location _____

Who you ran with _____

weather _____

How did you feel

Goal CompleteD?

Yes ◯ No ◯

Good ◯
Tired ◯
Sore ◯
fatigued ◯

Notes

Date _____

Training distance _____

Time run _____

Location _____

Who you ran with _____

weather _____

How did you feel

Good ◯
Tired ◯
Sore ◯
fatigued ◯

Goal Complete?

Yes ◯   No ◯

Notes

....
....
....
....
....
....
....
....
....

....
....
....
....

Date _____

Training distance _____

Time run _____

Location _____

Who you ran with _____

weather _____

How did you feel

Good ◯
Tired ◯
Sore ◯
fatigued ◯

Goal CompleteD?

Yes ◯   No ◯

Notes

....
....
....
....
....
....
....
....
....

....
....
....
....

Date _____

Training distance _____

Time run _____

Location _____

Who you ran with _____

weather _____

How did you feel

Good ◯

Tired ◯

Sore ◯

fatigued ◯

Goal Complete?

Yes ◯   No ◯

Notes

....
....
....
....
....
....
....
....

....
....
....
....

Date _____

Training distance _____

Time run _____

Location _____

Who you ran with _____

weather _____

How did you feel

Good ◯

Tired ◯

Sore ◯

fatigued ◯

Goal CompleteD?

Yes ◯   No ◯

Notes

....
....
....
....
....
....
....
....

....
....
....
....

Date

Training distance

Time run

Location

Who you ran with

weather

How did you feel

Goal Complete?

Yes ◯ No ◯

Good ◯
Tired ◯
Sore ◯
fatigued ◯

Notes

Date

Training distance

Time run

Location

Who you ran with

weather

How did you feel

Goal CompleteD?

Yes ◯ No ◯

Good ◯
Tired ◯
Sore ◯
fatigued ◯

Notes

Date _____

Training distance _____

Time run _____

Location _____

Who you ran with _____

weather _____

How did you feel

Goal Complete?

Yes ◯   No ◯

Good ◯
Tired ◯
Sore ◯
fatigued ◯

Notes

....
....
....
....
....
....
....
....
....

Date _____

Training distance _____

Time run _____

Location _____

Who you ran with _____

weather _____

How did you feel

Goal CompleteD?

Yes ◯   No ◯

Good ◯
Tired ◯
Sore ◯
fatigued ◯

Notes

....
....
....
....
....
....
....
....
....

Made in the USA
Monee, IL
13 April 2021